Macramé For Beginners

An Easy Step By Step Guide To Create Macrema

DEDICATION

GW00399899

Contents

I. Get Started with this Easy Beginner's Guide

Macrame is a decorative knotting craft that anyone can do with just a little bit of practice! It's is a great way to create beautiful and functional pieces of art to decorate your home with vintage flair. In this article, I'll show you the common macrame knots, recommend my favorite macrame materials, and show you how to start your first project. Keep reading to learn how to macrame with this easy step-by-step guide.

What is Macrame

Macrame is a creative knotting technique that can be used to make a variety of items, including jewelry and other decorative items. It's a great way to relax and create beautiful art pieces for your home. Macrame is traditionally made with cotton or hemp rope. The ropes are tied in different knots to create beautiful knotted patterns.

History of Macrame

The craft of macrame is believed to have originated with Arabic weavers during the 13th century, who used knotting techniques to create towels, shawls, and tapestries. From there, it spread across Europe and the rest of the work.

Macrame has been popular in many periods throughout history, including the Victorian Era, the 1970s, and now. Today, you'll see macrame being used to create modern wall hangings, plant hangers, friendship bracelets, belts, and bags.

How to Get Started with Macrame

It's easy to get started with macrame – all you need is some macrame cord and a little bit of practice.

This macrame beginner's guide will teach you everything you need to know to get started. I'll show you:

What Supplies You'll Need

How To Set Up Your Workspace

And How To Tie The Basic Macrame Knots.

Is macrame easy to learn?

Yes, macrame is easy to learn! Although it may look complicated at first glance, macrame is a simple craft that anyone can learn to do. Once you learn how to tie the basic macrame knots, you can combine them in different ways to create any pattern you can imagine.

Macrame Supplies

You don't need any complicated tools or expensive materials to do macrame. For most projects, you'll only need:

Rope

Scissors

Measuring Tape

You can make macrame with cords made from a variety of materials, including cotton, linen, hemp, jute, leather, or wool.

Some projects will require special hardware, like metal hoops, wooden rings, purse handles, or belt buckles.

You can add other decorative elements, like glass or wood beads.

Best Rope for Macrame

The best type of macrame cord is cotton twine or rope. Cotton rope is soft, flexible, and widely available. It's easy to tie, and it won't stretch out over time.

Cotton rope can be purchased online or at most craft stores for a reasonable price. For most home decor projects, I prefer to use a 4-6mm 3-ply cotton cord.

For jewelry projects (micro-macrame), choose a cord that is less than 2mm in diameter.

Other Materials

You can also use hemp rope or jute to give your projects a more rustic, natural look. These materials are slightly more challenging to work with, but they provide a durable and textured finished product. Other materials you can use include leather cord, nylon paracord, and polypropylene rope.

Can you use yarn for macrame?

You can use yarn for macrame, but it wouldn't be my first choice. The type of yarn that you'd normally use for knitting or crochet is usually too thin and stretchy. Most knitting yarns compress so much that the knots you'd make would be smaller than expected.

That said, you can use cotton yarn for small macrame projects since it's not as stretchy or compressible.

Setting up your Workspace

Before you start a new project, you'll need to set up a macrame workspace. Make sure you have adequate lighting and enough room to move around comfortably.

Depending on the type and size of your project, you can work horizontally on a flat surface, or vertically on a hanging setup.

Horizontal Setup

You can do some smaller projects on a flat, horizontal surface – like a tabletop. Secure the starting end of the piece to the table to keep tension on the cords as you work. For smaller pieces, like macrame bracelets, you can secure them underneath the clip of a clipboard.

Vertical Setup

Larger projects, especially wall hangings, will require a vertical workspace. Hang your work high enough that you can work comfortably.

Here are a few strategies for hanging your piece:

Hang a wood dowel rod from a clothing rack.

Over the back of a door

Over the back of a tall chair

From a doorknob

If you'll be making a lot of wall hangings, I highly recommend investing in a rolling garment rack.

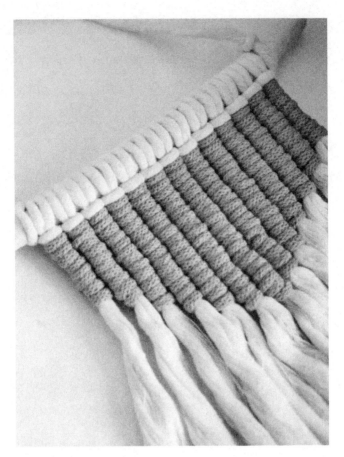

Basic Macrame Knots

Now that you have your materials and your workspace, you're ready to learn the basic macrame knotting techniques.

Macrame knots are easy to learn, but they do take some practice to truly master. Once you know these common macrame knots, you'll be able to recreate all of the beautiful projects you see online.

Here are the knots you'll need to know, broken down into four categories: mounting knots, square knots, hitch knots, and gathering knots.

Mounting Knots

Use mounting knots to attach your rope to a dowel rod or wooden ring.

Lark's Head Knot

The lark's head knot is a super simple knot used to attach your rope to a dowel rod, ring, or even another rope. It can be tied forward-facing or reverse-facing. Here's how to tie both:

To make a Lark's Head Knot:

Measure and cut a length of cord. Fold the rope in half, bringing the ends together.

Bring the folded loop up in front of the dowel, then back down behind the dowel. With the loop pointing downwards, pull the two ends of the cord through the loop.

Pull down on the ends to tighten the knot, making sure both ends are even.

Reverse Lark's Head Knot

To make a reverse lark's head knot:

Measure and cut a length of cord. Fold the rope in half.

Bring the folded loop up behind the dowel, then forward and down in front of the dowel. With the loop pointing downward, pull the ends of the rope up and through the loop.

Pull down on the ends to tighten the knot, making sure both ends are even.

Square Knots and Variations

Square Knots and Half Square Knots are versatile macrame knots that you'll use in almost every pattern.

This category of knots is made with four cords: two outer cords, called working cords, around two middle cords, called filler cords.

Half Square Knot

Cut two pieces of rope, and attach them to a wooden dowel with a lark's head knot. You will now have four strands of cord.

To make a half square knot:

Bring the left working cord over the two filler cords and under the right working cord.

Bring the right working cord under the two filler cords and up over the left working cord.

Tighten the knot.

Right Half Square Knot

This is the mirror image of the previous half square knot.

Bring the right working cord over the two filler cords and under the left cord.

Bring the left working cord under the two filler cords and up over the right cord.

Tighten the knot.

Square Knot

Each square knot is made from two half square knots, worked one after the other.

Square Knot, also called Left-facing Square Knot

Work a left half-square knot followed by a right half-square knot.

Right-Facing Square knot

Work a right half-square knot followed by a left half-square knot.

Half Knot Spiral

The spiral knot is a sequence of half-square knots worked one after another. Make sure all of the half square knots are facing the same way.

Hitches and Variations

This third category of knots makes beautiful designs but can be a bit trickier for beginners.

Half Hitch

The half hitch knot is a simple knot that can be combined in different ways. You can tie hitch knots with an existing project cord, or a new cord.

Double Half Hitch Knot, also called Clove Hitch Knot

This is a variation of the half hitch knot. It can be tied to create horizontal, vertical, and even diagonal lines in macrame pieces.

Horizontal Double Half Hitch

A row of horizontal double half hitch knots made a raised bar across your work. Each horizontal double half hitch knot is made from two half hitch knots made from the same working cord.

Diagonal Double Half Hitch Knot

Diagonal double half hitch knots are very similar to horizontal double half hitch knots, except the row of knots is positioned diagonally instead of horizontally.

Vertical Double Half-Hitch

A vertical double half hitch knot is made from two half hitch knots. To make vertical double half hitch knots, use one working cord to make double half hitch knots across multiple filler corder.

Gathering Knots

And finally, we have a group of knots that are used to finish projects.

Overhand Knot

The overhand knot is often used to prevent the end of a length of rope from unraveling. Overhand knots can also be used to tie two cords together at the bottom of a piece.

Wrapping Knot

Use a wrapping knot to secure a group of cords. You can use this knot at the beginning or end of a macrame project.

Cut a long length of cord. (You will trim it to size later.)

Gather the group of cords that need to be wrapped. Bring the folded end of the working cord down to the area you want to wrap.

Wrap the working cord around the grouped cords. Pass the working cord through the loop, and pull the other end to secure.

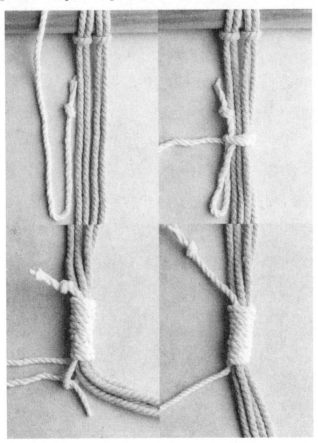

How to Add Fringe to Macrame

The type of fringe you can create depends on the type of cord you've used for the project.

Trim the cords to your desired length.

Use a stiff wire brush to brush the cords, starting and the ends and working up. Brushing the cords will separate the fibers to create a fine fringe.

Trim the ends again with sharp scissors.

Macrame Project Ideas

Here are a few different patterns and easy macrame projects you can try.

Start with smaller projects made with thinner cords.

Easy macrame plant hanger

Micro-macrame hemp bracelets

Macrame wall hanging

Cute macrame keychains

Later, try larger projects made with thicker cords.

Boho macrame table runner

Outdoor macrame hammock

Upcycled macrame circle chair

Macrame curtain

Frequently Asked Questions

Here are common questions that beginners ask when they first start to learn macrame.

What size cord should I use?

The right size cord will depend on the type of project. The smaller the string, the smaller the knots will be.

Larger home decor projects like wall hangings and plant holders require a sturdier rope. For these types of projects, choose a cord that is 4mm-6mm in diameter.

For smaller projects, like bracelets and necklaces, choose a soft, flexible cord that's less than 2mm in diameter.

For outdoor projects, like hammocks or chairs, consider a durable polypropylene rope.

How much rope do I need?

It can be hard to tell you exactly how much cord to buy. The length depends on the number and types of knots being tied on any given cord.

For example, filler cords that have few, if any, knots will be shorter than working cords.

But, as a general rule, allow yourself five or six times as much cord than the length of the projects. Add extra length if you want to make fringe at the bottom.

Remember that it's better to have too much rope than too little – you can always trim off the excess!

Why are my knots uneven?

Everyone struggles with uneven knots when they first start macrame. My more important tip is to keep your tension even while tying knots. Find the balance between knots that are too loose (too big) and too tight (too small).

Neat and tidy knots will come with practice. Keep going until your fingers get into a good rhythm.

II. Christmas Tree Wall Hanging

Materials

green macrame yarn (4mm)

ivory macrame yarn

wool brush

comb

wooden ring or star (I used a wooden gift tag that I altered)

measuring tape

scissors

wooden dowel rod (I had 5/8 rod left from my drawer pull tutorial)

yarn needle

battery operated fairy lights

fabric stiffener (optional)

You can customize this tree according to what you prefer. The sage green macrame yarn that I used is a bit pricey and I only used it because it was leftover. I'm sure you can find a cheaper option. You can also add beads to the spots where I added the yarn tassels. Or you can fill the entire macrame Christmas tree with tassels and not just the bottom like I did. I however wanted to show some of the macrame details and different knots which is why I didn't fill the entire tree with the tassels.

Like I said above, I used a wooden gift tag from Michael's and drilled big holes into it for the yarn. Since then I have found <u>the perfect star</u> that I could have bought instead.

Instructions

I love opening and combing macrame yarn. I love the process of it and I adore the look of it. Another example is my combed macrame yarn art. I definitely wanted to incorporate this look into my little Christmas tree.

The most asked question on any macrame tutorial is always: How much yarn did you use and how much do I need overall? And it's never a straight answer to me and here is why…

When I started this Christmas tree project, I wasn't exactly sure how big I wanted to make the tree but I knew that if I had a lot of scraps at the end when trimming the fringe I'd use that for the tassels so I wasn't worried about using too much yarn.

If you use a cheaper macrame yarn than mine that is maybe 3mm or 5mm then you maybe need a different length or amount. So that's something to keep in mind as well.

If you want to make it a bit bigger than mine then you will obviously also need longer pieces of yarn.

My Yarn Measurements

20 pieces of yarn (I cut mine all at 160 inches long which will leave you with a lot of scraps in the end. As I said, this is fine because they are needed for the tassels. It is more complicated if you calculate and subtract inches to make them shorter as you progress on the tree.)

yarn for 10 tassels (6 pieces of string per tassel at 8 inches long = 60 pieces of yarn at 8 inches long altogether)

8 pieces of ivory yarn at 16" inches long

Step-By-Step Photos

Creating The Body Of The Christmas Tree

I started out by folding two 160-inch pieces of macrame yarn in half and looping them onto the holes in the wooden star with Lark's Head knots

Then I taped the star with duct tape to my kitchen counter.

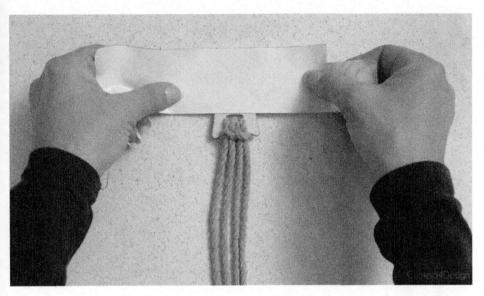

The entire macrame Christmas tree pattern is basically made with diagonal Double Half Hitch knots (some also call them diagonal Clove Hitch Knot but there is a slight difference in the yarn piece actually crossing in the back). Half Hitch Knots are loops placed onto another piece of yarn or in this case also at the bottom of the tree onto the dowel rod.

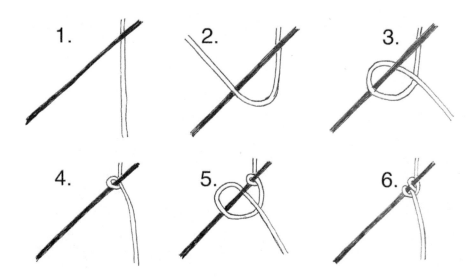

Here you can see exactly how the loops are formed

Make two Half Hitch knots right after the loops on the star.

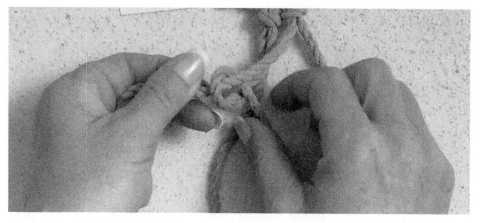

And then add one 160 inch piece of yarn folded in half onto the left and right side.

In this case for the macrame Christmas tree, you have to keep adding yarn pieces to make the tree shape wider towards the bottom.

Add the strings with reversed Lark's Head knots. It's the same looping technique used when adding the yarn to the star but this time just turned around so you don't see the loop.

Then it's time to add another row of diagonal Half Hitch knots

31

followed by adding more yarn pieces.

The below image is a guide to show where the extra yarn was added.

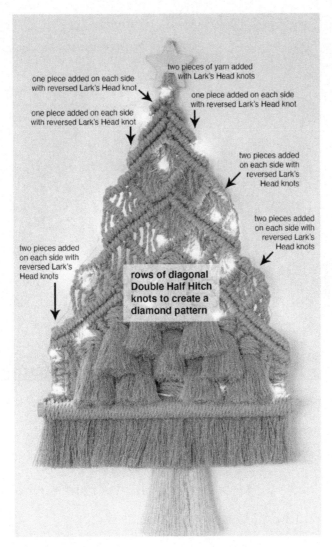

two pieces of yarn added with Lark's Head knots

one piece added on each side with reversed Lark's Head knot

one piece added on each side with reversed Lark's Head knot

one piece added on each side with reversed Lark's Head knot

two pieces added on each side with reversed Lark's Head knots

two pieces added on each side with reversed Lark's Head knots

two pieces added on each side with reversed Lark's Head knots

rows of diagonal Double Half Hitch knots to create a diamond pattern

At this point, I added an extra loop of Half Hitch knots after the reversed Lark's Head knots on each side to make the tree a bit wider without adding the yarn. Let me show you what I mean…

a Half Hitch knot to the right of the reversed Lark's Head knot and then repeat on the left side

I repeated the same row another time.

After that, I added another row of diagonal Half Hitch Knots followed by two 160" pieces on each side.

When I had 24 strings hanging down, I decided it was time to add the diamond pattern. Separate the yarn into 3 groups of 8.

Time to make the diamond pattern.

It doesn't look like it in the below photo, but the diamond center has 6 strings on the inside. I took that as a guide for the rest of them.

After that create diamonds all the way down. In the end, I had 4 diamonds at the bottom. Keep adding the rows of diamonds with the help of the above description until you have the desired length of the tree.

Three times I added a second row of diagonal Half Hitch Knots to add some interest but that's also optional. Below you can see one of those double rows.

At the end, I added square knots to even out the rows before adding the dowel rod.

I don't have a set number of knots that I used because some needed more than other strands to make it all look even and hang the rod straight as you can see in the above image.

Attach the dowel rod to the macrame Christmas tree wallhanging by looping the 40 hanging strings into Half Hitch knots again around the rod. Since you cut 20 pieces of yarn at the beginning and then folded them in half to add them into the piece, you now ended up with 40 strings.

I opened and combed the bottom fringe. This is where you can soak the fringe in starch, let it dry and then comb and trim the ends which is what I did.

Depending on the type of yarn the ends curl a lot after opening and the starch helps prevent that.

I added the starch to the bottom fringe and ivory tassel but not the rest.

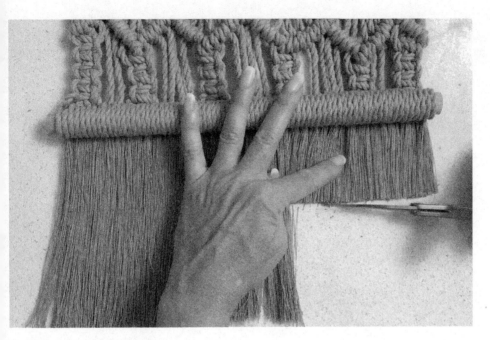

Adding The Tassels

Below I'm showing you one piece of yarn in a contrasting color so you can see how all the tassels were formed on the macrame Christmas tree. This is exactly the same way I added the wool in my macrame wreath tutorial.

That is how you add the ivory tassel that creates the tree trunk of the macrame Christmas tree.

Cut 8 pieces of ivory yarn at 16 inches long, fold them in half and loop them through the bottom center.

And it is exactly the same way that I added the green tassels afterward too. I opened and comb all the yarn but didn't add any starch.

Open and comb the yarn and after that trim the tassels. Mine are about 2.5 inches long.

Adding The Fairy Lights

Lastly, I tied the battery pack of the fairy lights to the back of the

tree. Then I threaded the lights through the tree using the wool

needle. You don't really need the needle but I felt like it made it

easier for sure.

Below you can see the exact measurements of my tree.

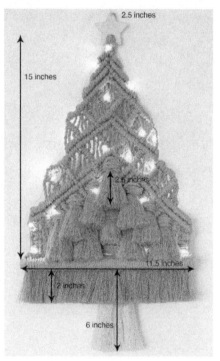

Finished Macrame Christmas Tree

I really love how this little Christmas tree turned out and looks amongst all my other macrame decor. It has definitely become a hobby of mine to work with yarn.

III. Macrame Earrings

Materials

macrame cord (I use this macrame yarn but you could use different

cord colors)

sharp scissors (I like using hair cutting scissors for my craft projects)

comb or brush

small hoop earrings (different hoop earrings sizes available, mine are about 50mm)

Clip or something else to clip the earring to. I used a chop stick and clip or you could use a clothing pin

fabric stiffener

Instructions

I decided to use the simple knots called Square Knots and for these macrame earrings, I only needed 3 Square Knots per earring.

Above you can see all my scraps which I started out by opening up the strands. They come apart into 4 strands.

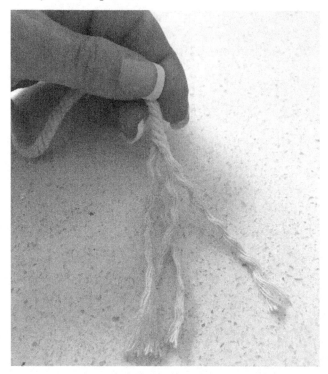

I laid them out on a flat surface and gathered two of them for the top loops on the earrings. The reason that I opened them beforehand is that I liked the look better and because I didn't want to take the entire strand to make the earrings lighter in weight.

I looped them over the hoop earring with Lark's Head Knots which is also the way you start any macrame wallhanging.

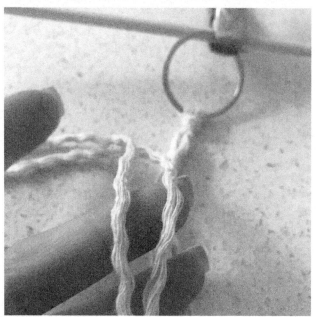

Above you can see the two strands and below I'm showing you how the loop is formed. It's super easy.

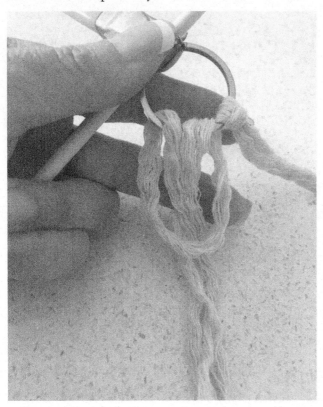

I used 4 looped strands of 2 for each hoop as you can see below:

After that is where the square knots come into place.

How To Make A Macrame Square Knot

The key for the square knot is that you alternate which string you overlay in the foreground. If you don't alternate then you will make a spiral knot which I also use and love but didn't want for this project.

How to make a simple macrame square
knot

Below is exactly the three Square Knot configuration that I attached

to the hoops. I'm showing it to you in a loose version so you can see the way it is set up better. For the DIY macrame earrings, I pulled everything tight though.

Below are two square knots:

And then you make the third square knot in the middle as you can see below:

In the end, you just comb the open ends and give them a haircut to come up with your desired shape of the macrame earrings.

Photos of finished macrame earrings

I wanted mine to have a fanned shape but you could make them long and straight or even give them a triangular shape.

I love them and have worn them many times already. I have really stretched out ear loops and I have found something that helps me wear big earrings again.

I buy these <u>clear ear stickers</u> and apply them to the back of my earlobe before sticking the actual earring through my ear holes. They work like a charm!

IV. Cat Bed

This DIY cat bed was a true evolution from a differently planned project to the outcome which I will get to in a bit. I have been wanting to make a hanging DIY cat bed for our dining room window because the windowsill is so small and the cats love sitting there to watch the birds that nest in our shutters. We don't have enough room for a cat tree though, so a hanging macrame bed was my idea for solving this problem and this hanging DIY cat bed is actually pretty similar to my macrame plant hanger

Materials

macrame cord

scissors

two 18-inch metal hoops

wood beads are optional (I already had mine and can't find the exact same ones but THESE would be great or THESE, THESE and THESE)

18-inch round pillow (or HERE)

plant hook to mount to the wall

measuring tape

small clamps optional

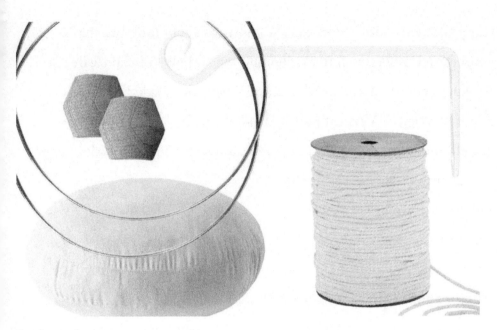

Instructions

How To Wrap The Hoops With Macrame Cord

I started out by wrapping the two brass rings with Vertical Lark's Head Knots which is definitely optional. You can make it even easier if you don't mind the shiny gold. I, on the other hand didn't want the brass to show and also wanted to make sure that the other parts didn't slide around on the brass which wrapping the rings accomplishes. You could also use a dab of hot glue under the parts of the macrame yarn that are attached to the hoops to avoid sliding if you want to skip the hoop wrapping part.

Cut a string around 40 feet long. I know it's super long but that's what I used. I bunch all the string into a neat ball so I can easily loop the knots and then just pull out more whenever needed.

Start creating the Vertical Lark's Head Knots by looping the yarn around the hoop as shown in the first and second photo with a short end of string hanging to the side

Pull the yarn tight

Then lay the yarn on top of the ring and pull through the back to the left side and pull tight

After that place the yarn behind the loop and up through the left as pictured. (I always keep telling myself in my head first front over and trough the back, then behind over and through the front so I remember to alternate to create the Vertical Lark's Head Knots)

When you reach all the way around, you can cover the small string that you left at the beginning of the wrapping with more Vertical Lark's Head Knots.

At the end you will have one piece of string left hanging which you will cover later with the other knots of the hanging cat bed.

If you run out of string during the hoop wrapping, you can just cover the ending string the same way and start a new row of Knots the way

I showed you at the beginning.

Do this with both 18-inch hoops and put them aside until later.

Creating The Hanging Part Of The Macrame Diy Cat Bed

The way I created the loop part to hang the cat bed can be done different ways. If you want to save time then you can do it with a ring the way. Just make sure you use a <u>metal ring</u> instead because the wooden rings can snap and break.

The loop I created is again the same Vertical Lark's Head knots that I used to wrap the hoops. This time you wrap the strings that hang down at the center with a piece of yarn that's about 8-foot long.

Figuring Out How Much Macrame Yarn To Use

To me figuring out how much yarn to use is always the hardest part, especially when it is a project that I come up with myself and I'm not following someone else's tutorial. I'd rather end up with a lot of leftover yarn material than not having enough.

You need to determine how long you want the cat bed to hang down. I knew that I wanted the bed to hang slightly above the windowsill. So I hung my plant hook above the window first and then measured the length.

I multiplied that times 10 so I could have enough yarn for the

rest of the knotting and the bottom tassel part.

Cut 8 pieces of yarn of that length and fold in half.

After I folded the yarn in half I draped the center part over a doorknob to start the Vertical Lark's Head Knots at the center of the folded yarn with the separate 8-foot piece of yarn.

Now simply repeat the same steps for the Vertical Lark's Head Knots as I showed you above when wrapping the hoops

Like I mentioned earlier my <u>macrame lantern tutorial</u> pretty much starts out the same way except for the ring part.

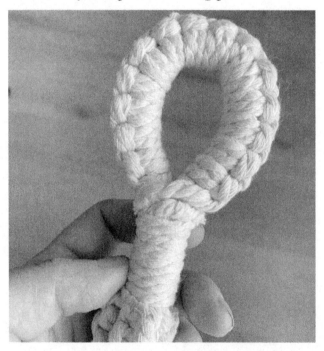

The Gathering Knot Method is best. Or you can just tie it of by twisting yarn around the strands and placing a tight standard knot at the end to hold it all in place.

For the rest of the project I used only square knots but you could also use spiral knots which are almost the same as the square knots, you just don't alternate.

How to make a simple macrame square
knot

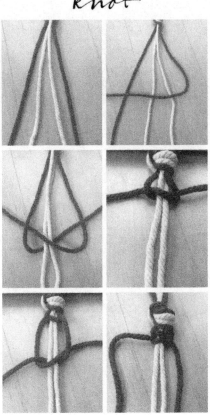

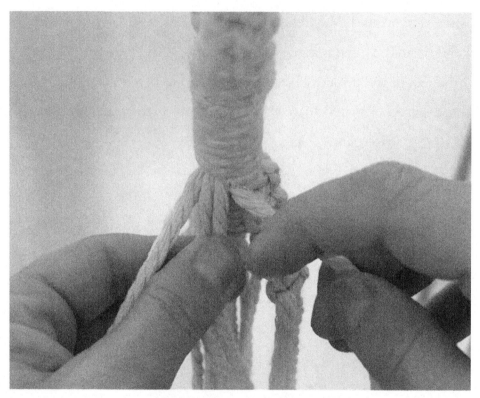

I decided to not use Square Knots the entire string sections to make the project faster and to make it more visually interesting which is also why I added the wooden beads.

Below you can see that I always measured 5-inch equal sections on all 4 parts of the strands and just kept repeating that.

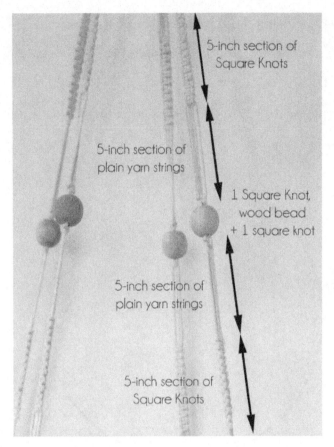

5-inch section of
Square Knots

5-inch section of
plain yarn strings

1 Square Knot,
wood bead
+ 1 square knot

5-inch section of
plain yarn strings

5-inch section of
Square Knots

My beads didn't have a hole big enough to add 4 strands of macrame yarn so I used a 3/8 drill bit to make the existing holes big enough. I clamped the beads into a vice and then drilled into the center. This leaves little teeth marks from the vice but I'm ok with that since I don't have a drill press.

Attaching The Hoops To The Hanging Strands

It's time to create the area for the pillow to create the lounging part of the cat bed.

I marked 4 equal sections on the hoops and attached the strands with square knots to the hoop

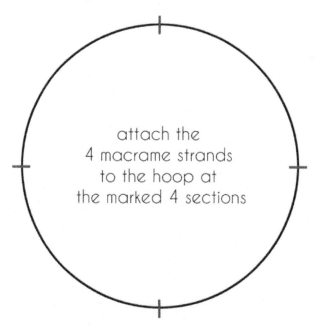

attach the
4 macrame strands
to the hoop at
the marked 4 sections

Place the two center strands in front of the hoop and the two outside ones behind the hoop and then place the square knot under the hoop to hold it all in place.

Now it is time to cut more string for the sections between the top hanging strands. I decided to do three more strands for a Square Knot grid in between.

Cut 24 pieces of macrame yarn at 180 inches long. You need to fold each strand in half and loop them onto the hoop with a Lark's Head Knot the way I showed you above when starting the Vertical Lark's Head Knots. The only difference is that there isn't just a small piece of yarn hanging to the side. This time it is equal yarn parts because you folded it in half.

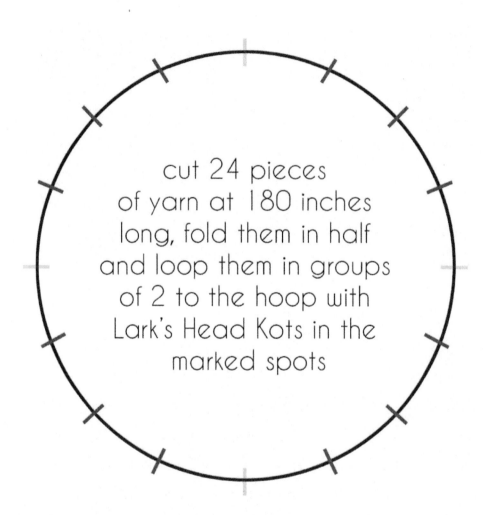

cut 24 pieces
of yarn at 180 inches
long, fold them in half
and loop them in groups
of 2 to the hoop with
Lark's Head Kots in the
marked spots

Believe it or not, I eyeballed this part instead of marking it exactly because in the end you won't be able to tell.

Like I said above, fold the strands in half and loop the macrame yarn onto the hoop with Lark's Head Knots as shown below

Each section has two Lark's Head Knots to get the 4 strands that are always needed to create Square Knots.

I added a Square Knot to each section to match the Square Knots I used to attach the top hanging strands to the hoop.

Here you can see a finished row

Repeat this 12 times to complete all the sections.

Time To Make The Grid That Will Eventually Hold The Pillow For The Cat To Sleep On.

Grab the two outside strands on two adjacent sections and gather them with a Square Knot. I measured about two inches down. Then keep repeating this all the way around the perimeter of the hoop.

Next, you have to repeat that again to create a criss-cross pattern.

Grab the two adjacent strands next to each other which you can see below and gather with another Square Knot.

You have to attach the second hoop with more Square Knots which is the same way you attached the first hoop, remember?

Next you could continue the grid knotting with Square Knots to meet in the center of the hoop the way I did above but I decided to just gather the strands and tie them together to make things easier for me and you.

I simply used a piece of macrame yarn to tightly knot the yarn strands together in the center. You could also use a Gathering Knot like I used at the top of the DIY cat bed.

Trim the tassel at the bottom of the hanging DIY cat bed, add the pillow and you are done.

How To Hang A Macrame Cat Bed

My hanging planters are usually all hung from the curtain rods which has worked well but for the macrame cat bed I wanted to ensure that it was hung a bit sturdier.

I used a planter hook that is typically used outside to hang the cat bed as you can see below. This way I could use two large screws to drill into the wooden structure that holds the window behind the drywall. It might not look as pretty but I better play it safe than be sorry later. Our kitties safety always comes first!

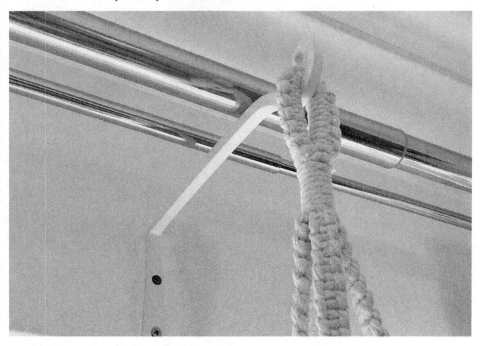

Finished hanging DIY cat bed

Willy happily modeled the DIY cat bed for you. He loves the

attention when I take photos of him. So cute!

V. Flush Mount Macrame Light Fixture

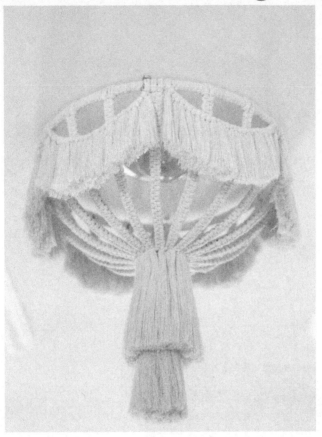

Materials To Make Light Fixture

macrame cord

metal hanging basket (I bought the 18-inch one but you could buy

the smaller 16-inch one or even go larger if you'd like)

sharp craft scissors

comb

fabric stiffener

hair straightening iron

nail

The reason I bought this particular wire basket is that it doesn't have metal loops at the top to hang the chain from. If you bought a metal basket with little loops then you have to take metal snippers and cut them off.

Instructions To Make Light Fixture

Wrapping The Top Part Of The Hanging Basket With

Macrame Yarn

First, you have to remove the moss from the wire hanging basket.
Mine was simply attached with a bunch of plastic straps that you
could easily snip off.

I didn't write down the length of the piece I used to wrap the top of
the basket (45 feet should be enough) because it was a long scrap
piece I had. You can even use small scrap pieces of yarn, but you
need to make sure that they always end and start at one of the metal
sections that run down to the center, so you can later hide the ends
under one of the Square Knots.

I used Vertical Lark's Head Knots to wrap the top part and it is the
same method that I used to wrap the metal hoops in my macrame cat
bed tutorial as well. That tutorial has a nice slow layout of the knots
with photos

Make sure to do these knots nice and tight so non of the black metal
shows.

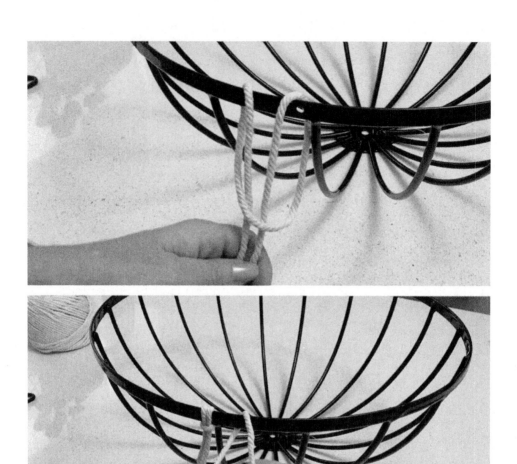

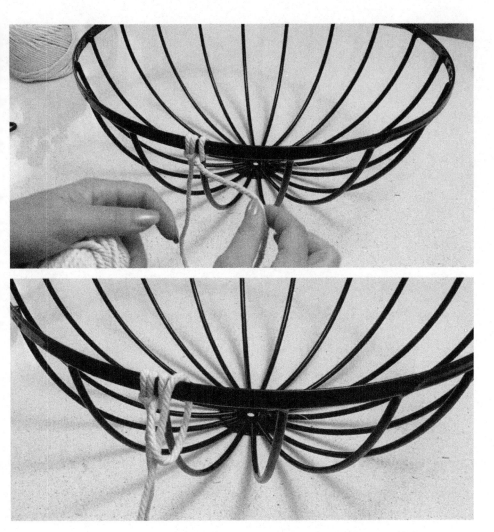

Keep repeating these looped Vertical Lark's Head Knots all the way around the perimeter of the metal basket structure.

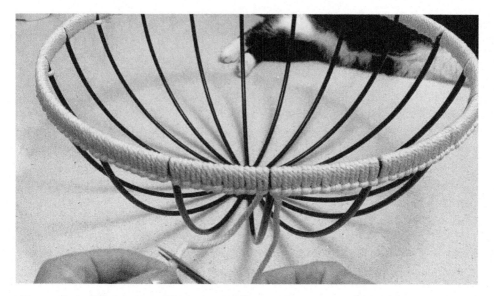

Wrapping The Metal Sections That Run From Top To Bottom Of The Basket

For that part I used square knots again which I use in a lot of my tutorials.

I needed 220-inch pieces times 4 per metal section and my basket has 18 metal sections running from top to bottom, so I needed 72 pieces of macrame yarn at 220-inches long.

Below you can see the short beginning and end pieces of macrame strings hanging down from wrapping the top. Next is how you can hide them under the rows of square knots. You just need to make sure they remain close to the metal strand.

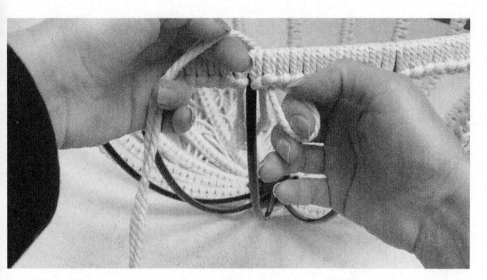

Fold one of those 220-inch strands in half and loop them onto the basket top with a Lark's Head knot to the right side of a metal strand. And repeat that with another strand to the left side of the metal strand.

This gives you the 4 strands of macrame yarn needed for Square Knots.

Let me show you again how the square knot is made if you are new around here. The below light colors strands would be the one that you keep in front of the metal strand/rod going down and the dark ones are the outer two yarn strands that do the wrapping and knotting. This way you can hide the black metal well. They also hide the end yarn pieces from wrapping the top of the baskets.

How to make a simple macrame square
knot

Below you can see nicely how the short end yarn pieces will be

hidden under the knots.

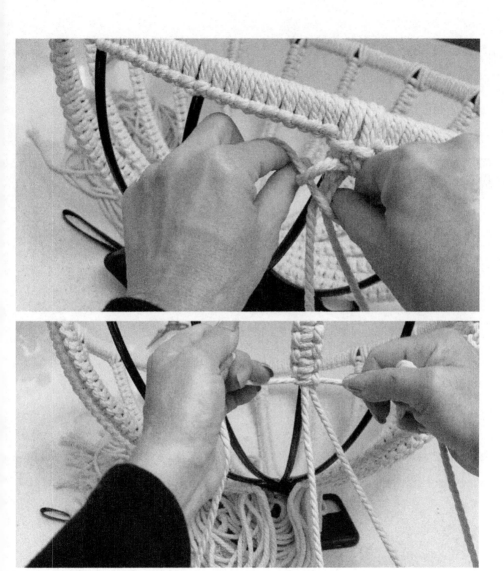

Keep repeating the Square Knots all the way to the bottom of the metal basket. When I came to the bottom part, turned the basket around. This part can get a little bit more challenging to maneuver because the area is a little tight. You'll get the hang of it.

Let the left over macrame yarn hang at the bottom because that is what will form the tassel at the end.

Below it the metal basket with all sections wrapped in square knots.

Creating The Fringed And Draped Sections Of The Macrame Light Fixture

I cut 6 pieces of macrame yarn at 24 inches long for the swag parts and cut a pile of 10-inch pieces of yarn from the mountains of scrap pieces that I have left from other projects. Those small pieces will create the fringe.

Remember how you start the vertical Lark's Head Knots and Lark's Head Knot above? This is how you will also attach the 24-inch pieces of yarn. See below...

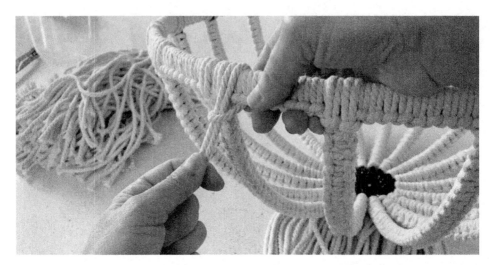

Then I skipped two of the metal strands wrapped in Square Knots and attached the yarn to the basket top with another Vertical Lark's Head Knot. The swag section of the strand that hangs down is about 10 inches long.

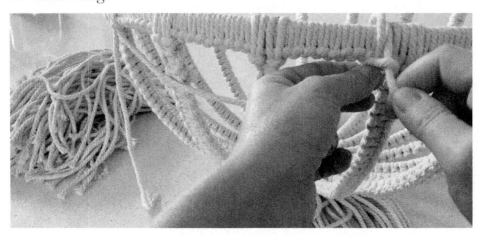

Next fold the 10-inch scrap pieces in half and loop it on the the draped macrame piece with more Lark's Head Knots.

Keep repeating this to fill the entire draped strand.

I love the look of unraveled macrame yarn because it creates a contrast to the twisted standard macrame yarn texture. This is definitely just optional and if you don't want to go through the work of opening up and combing all the yarn then just leave it. It still looks pretty. This counts for the tassel portion of the project too. That part makes the project definitely more time-consuming.

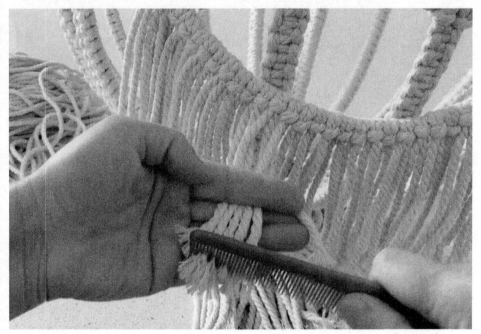

Below you can see one of the draped swags with all the macrame yarn unraveled and combed before trimming it.

Repeat this all the way around the macrame light fixture with more fringe-filled swags.

99

After this, I decided to hang the macrame light fixture from a curtain rod with some macrame yarn simply knotted to it so I could see where to trim the pieces. I cut mine to a length of 4 inches.

Next I opened the bottom strands hanging from the fixture. This part is time-consuming and you can just leave it be if you'd prefer that. For this part, I find that spraying on fabric stiffener and drying that with a straightening iron until it is dry helps the strands hand nice, straight, and stiff. It is a tad bit more difficult to untangle and straighten those long pieces.

Creating this macrame light fixture goes much faster if you skip the steps of unraveling the macrame yarn.

I wanted to do a stacked tassel at the bottom, so I cut 22 pieces of macrame yarn at 27 inches long and tied that off at the center with a small piece of yarn as shown below.

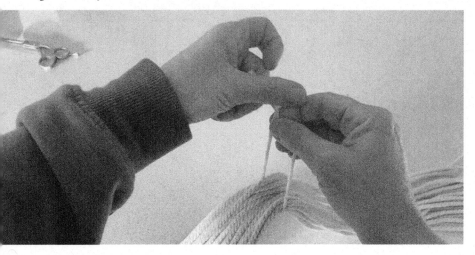

After that you need to thread the tied off tassel string through the first tassel and wire basket center and either tie a fat knot or tie the string to a nail/stick so the second tassel can't fall through the center. (see below)

You can either leave the string as is again to contrast the top fringe of the stacked tassel or open it the way I did.

Here are my measurements of what I trimmed the tassels to. Longer would also look good depending on where you want the fixture to hang.

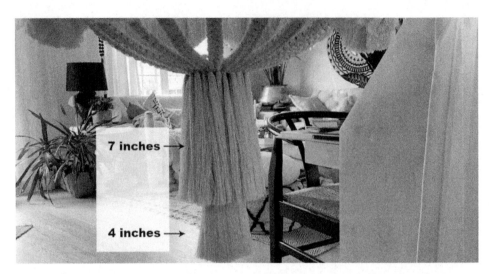

That's it! Now all you need to do is find a spot for this pretty boho flush mount light and hang. It can cover a variety of ugly standard ceiling lights like boob lights and recessed lighting.

Materials Needed For Hanging

drywall anchors and screws

#10 finishing washers

wire (any strong bendable wire will do)

You might be wondering what we had hanging in this spot before I searched everywhere for a before photo but I couldn't find one. I had a screw in pendant light converter with a glass Ikea shade which looked nice but it was hanging rather low and my husband kept banging things into the glass. I like the look and practicality now much better.

Start out by holding the macrame light fixture to the ceiling so you can lightly trace the inner and outer circumferences.

Below you can see the slight circle I drew from tracing the macrame light fixture on the ceiling. I did inside and outside perimeter because I wanted to place the screws more on the inside of the circle to avoid having the anchors and screws from showing.

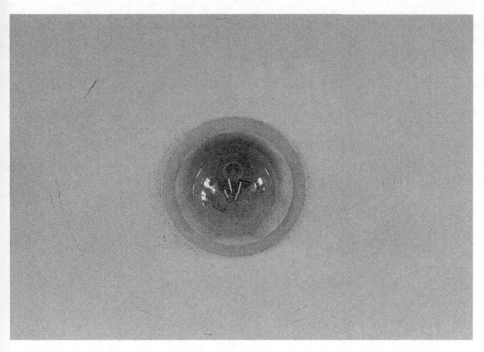

Originally, I had considered replacing the ugly recessed light with a converter and new cheap boob light but when the macrame light fixture was up on the ceiling I noticed that you couldn't really tell what was under all the macrame and so it didn't really matter anymore.

I wasn't worried about messing up the ceiling because if and when I ever replace this light, I will just use a ceiling medallion to cover the holes up. It looks nice and that way I don't have to patch and paint the ceiling. "I love painting ceilings," said nobody ever. LOL, am I right? I definitely hate painting ceilings!

Thread the washer onto the screw and tightly twist a wire that was folded in half around the screw behind the washer the way you can see below.

Hammer in the plastic anchor until you reach the spiral screw section and then screw the rest in with a screwdriver.

Next screw in the screw-wire-washer contraption you made earlier.

I decided to use 4 screw setups like this marked on the light fixture

circle as pictured below.

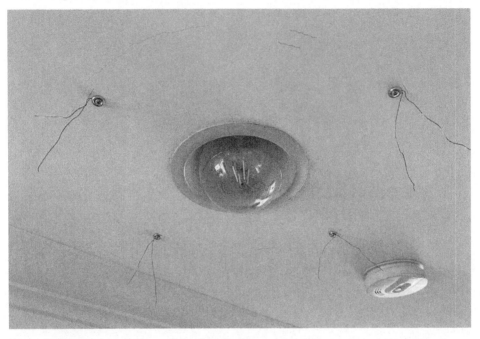

Place the macrame light fixture against the ceiling so you can wrap

the wire around the top.

Next twist the wire tightly around the top of the macrame light fixture in all 4 screw sections and hide the wire behind the macrame lamp shade.

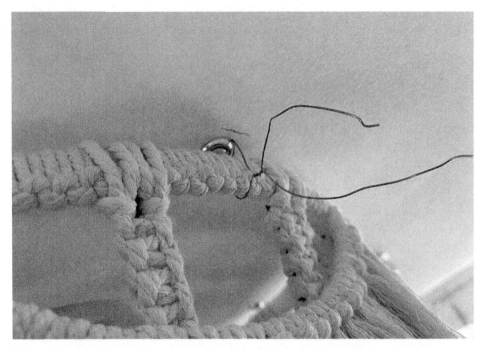

And voila, you have a pretty boho flush mount light fixture that barely cost you anything.

VI. Chandelier

Materials

cotton macrame cord

metal hanging basket (I bought the 18-inch one but you could buy
the smaller 16-inch one or even go larger if you'd like)

sharp craft scissors

comb

fabric stiffener

hair straightening iron

nail

fairy light fixture or another lighting kit

metal clips are optional to help you attach cords

Instructions

114

First Part Of The Macrame Chandelier

The first part of this tutorial is the same as my macramé flush mount light fixture.

For this part, you only need Vertical Lark's Head knots for the top and Square Knots for the side strands. If you measure and cut a piece of macrame yarn 45 feet long, it should be enough to wrap the top part.

You might have different measurements and amounts of metal strands depending on what basket you bought. I needed 220-inch pieces times 4 per metal section. There are 18 metal sections in my basket which meant I needed 72 pieces of macrame yarn at 220 inches long to wrap them all. I know that's a lot!

This macrame chandelier tutorial would have gotten way too long had I described the exact same steps again. If you need more details then head on over to the macrame flush mount light fixture for more in-depth descriptions.

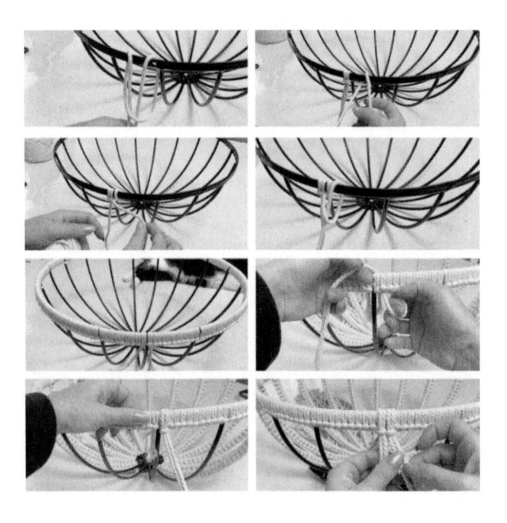

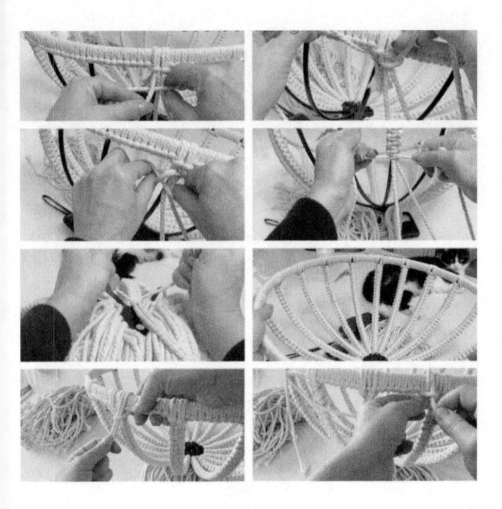

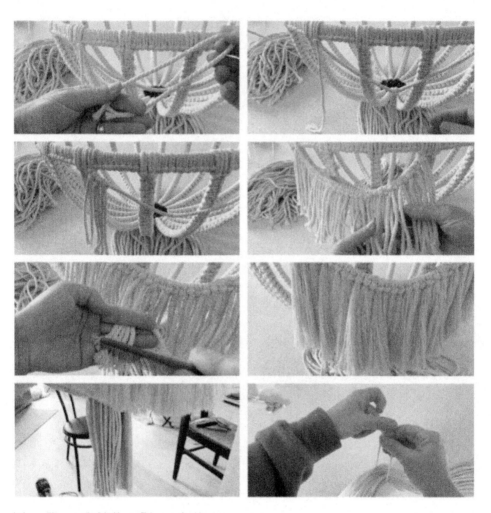

Top Part Of The Chandelier

For the top, I started out with the same looped and knotted hoop

that I used in my macrame cat bed tutorial. As I stated in that tutorial, you don't have to do it that way and could use a metal ring instead to save time. I personally like how it looks all knotted and uniform for this macrame chandelier. It's certainly preferential.

Cut 24 pieces of macrame yarn at 180 inches long and fold them in half over something like a doorknob.

Cut another piece of 8-foot macrame yarn to wrap the 24 pieces of macrame with Vertical Lark's Head Knots which were also used to wrap the top part of the metal basket earlier.

Fold the wrapped part in half and use the Gathering Knot Method to tightly wrap everything together to form an eyelet for hanging.

Then I hung that eyelet onto a broomstick that I propped up between barstools so I could work on the rest of the strands. Since you folded the 24 strands of macrame yarn in half, you now have 48 strands hanging down.

I sectioned those strands into groups of 4 strings, so I could stack rows of Square Knots again as I showed you earlier while wrapping the metal strands on the basket. You will end up with 12 strands of Square Knots that I made 2 inches long.

After that, I connected two strands of Square Knots with Alternating Square Knots. This way you'll end up with 6 strands of macrame Square Knot rows. Let me show you how…

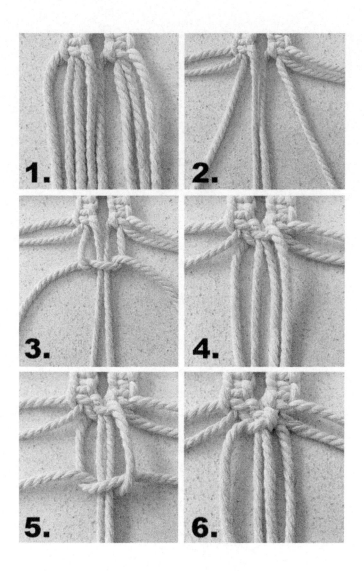

1. Line up the 8 strands of macrame yarn
2. Hold the two centerpieces of macrame yarn together so you can form the first row of square knots around them
3. Use the two adjacent pieces of yarn to the middle strands for the first Square Knot loop
4. Pull tight
5. Form the second Square Knot loop
6. Pull tight again and you can see that this Square Knot now connected the two stacked strands of Square Knots from earlier
7. Now you do the same thing to the left side with 4 strands
8. Be careful not to pull everything too tight or the Square Knots won't be straight across a horizontal line
9. Form the same Square Knot on the right side
10. Now repeat the square Knot in the center again
11. Keep going until you have a strand of Alternating Square Knots that is 11 inches long as you can see below on the finished piece.

Doesn't the below finished top piece look like an octopus? All you have to do now is knot it to the bottom lamp shade part of the light fixture.

2 inches of Square Knots
11 inches of Alternating Square Knots

Connecting The Top Part To The Bottom Part Of The Chandelier

The six arms that will carry the bottom part of the basket are knotted onto the top rim. For that I used square knots followed by diagonal clove hitch knots.

Macramé For Beginners

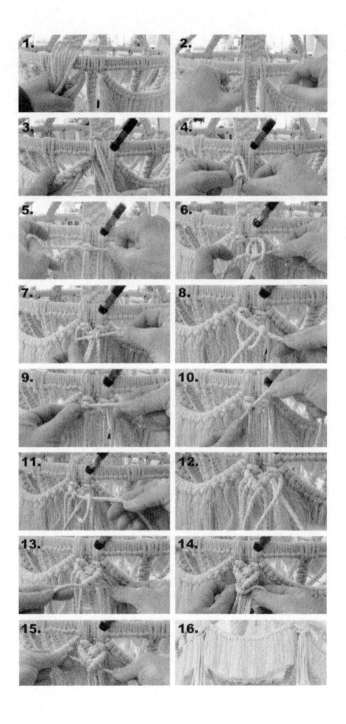

1. Hang the top part that looks like an octopus to something like a curtain rod and so you can prepare to attach the alternating square knot strands to the sections of the chandelier where the fringe swags meet. (this is where the clips can help you hang it all)

2. I folded the 4 strands behind the metal top and 4 in front as shown in image number 2. (first one behind, two in front, two behind, two in front, and last one behind again)

3. Time to attach the strands with Square Knots again. So grab the 4 left pieces of macrame yarn.

4. Form the first part of a Square Knot and pull very tight so it can hold the weight of the metal basket.

5. Pull the second part of the Square Knot tight as well.

6. Repeat the same thing on the right side with the other 4 strands formed into a tight Square Knot.

7. Form one Alternate Square Knot in the center.

8. Now it's time for the Diagonal Clove Hitch Knots. Grab the left outside strand and hold it down along the side of the Square Knots. Loop the next macrame piece onto that diagonally held piece of yarn.

9. Pull tight!

10. Repeat the same loop and pull tight again. Drop that strand and grab the next strand of macrame yarn in line from the Square Knots.

11. Repeat the same looping as above twice and drop the yarn to grab the next one in line. When you did this with 3 strands of yarn, you arrive at the center.

12. Repeat the same thing on the right side.

13. When you arrive at the center, the Diagonal Clove Hitch Knots form something that looks like a triangle.

14. Cut a small piece of yarn and tie the macrame yarn that hangs down together.

15. Hide the knot in the back.

16. Repeat this with all 6 arms and trim the yarn to about 6 inches long. I decided to not unravel those strands like the other fringe because I like the contrast to the unraveled fringe. You could certainly unravel and comb it too though.

Adding A Light To Your Macrame Chandelier

I'm sure you are wondering what you could use to light the macrame chandelier. I used a battery-operated fairy-light fixture I found on

Amazon but if you have a hardwired option in your ceiling then you can certainly just use a simple lighting kit.

I simply tied the fairy-lights to the center top part with another piece of macrame yarn and let the battery part rest in the center of the basket part. You can barely see it. The remote that comes with the light makes turning it on and off super easy.

Printed in Great Britain
by Amazon

27277929R00076